ONE MAN COOKING

Over 100 recipes, with many short cuts, for those cooking mainly for themselves or who want to improve their cooking

Shaun Dowling

Copyright © Shaun Dowling 2014

This book is sold subject to the condition that it shall not, by way of trade or otherwise, be lent, resold, hired out, or otherwise circulated without the publisher's prior consent in any form of binding or cover other than that in which it is published and without a similar condition including this condition being imposed on the subsequent publisher.

The moral right of Shaun Dowling has been asserted.

ISBN: **1499659156**
ISBN-13: **978-1499659153**

RECIPE INDEX

SIMPLE STARTERS AND PÂTÉS

Asparagus	7
Avocado vinaigrette	7
Crudités	7
Egg Mayonnaise	7
Hors d'oeuvres	8
Lumpfish Caviar	8
Melon	8
Parma Ham	8
Pâté Mackerel Pâté	10
Pâté Chicken Liver	10
Potted Shrimps	8
Prawn Cocktail	8
Rollmops	8
Quails Eggs	9
Salads (see Section 3)	16
Smoked Cod's Roe	9
Smoked Mackerel	9
Smoked Salmon	9
Whitebait	9

SOUPS

Haddock Chowder	11
Bacon and Vegetable Soup	12
Lentil and Potato Soup	12
Spinach, Pea and Stilton Soup	14
Lobster Chowder	14

SALADS

Salad Options	*16*
Egg Salad	*17*
Greek Salad	*17*
Salade Niçoise	*18*

EGGS AND CHEESE

Scrambled Eggs and Smoked Salmon	*20*
Omelettes	*21*
Cheese Soufflé	*21*
Tortilla (Spanish Omelette)	*22*
Oeufs Florentine	*22*

FISH

Grilled and Sautéed Fish	*24*
Kedgeree	*25*
Sole Meunière	*25*
Sole Mornay	*27*
Lobster Bisque Mélange	*27*
Fish Casserole	*28*
Light Tuna Curry	*28*
Flaked Cod in Cheese Sauce	*30*
Battered Haddock and Chips	*30*
Bouillabaisse	*31*
Smoked Haddock and Egg Mornay	*31*
Tuna Wok	*32*
Prawns and Spaghetti	*34*
Spanish Paella	*36*
Asian Prawns	*36*
Scallops, Ham and Beans	*37*
Fish Marsala	*37*
Moules Marinière	*38*

PASTA AND PIZZAS

Linguine in Pasta Sauce	40
Linguine alla Carbonara	41
Spaghetti Bolognese	41
Linguine, Cheese and Eggs	42
Linguine with Mussels and Clams	45
Macaroni Cheese	45
Seafood Linguine	46
Pizzas	46

CHICKEN

Thai Chicken	48
Chicken Curry	50
Chicken, Pepper and Tomatoes	50
Chicken in Black Bean Sauce	51
Coq au Vin	51
Chicken Casserole	52
Asian Chicken	53
Chicken Valentine	53
Chicken in Pasta Sauce	56
Chicken Paprika	56
Chicken in Mushroom Sauce	58
Chicken Leftovers	58

BEEF

Steak and French Fries	59
Boeuf Bourguignon	61
Beef Curry	61
Minute Steak and Mashed Potato	62
Beef Casserole	64
Carbonade Flamande	64
Beef Stroganoff	65
Stuffed Pepper	67
Boeuf Boulangère	67

Chilli con Carne	*68*
Boeuf à la Bonne Femme	*70*
Steak Tartare	*70*
Veal Stew	*71*
Steak au Poivre	*71*
Wiener Schnitzel	*73*
Corned Beef Hash	*73*
Calves' Liver and Bacon	*74*

LAMB

Lamb Curry	*76*
Quick Cassoulet	*78*
Lamb's Liver, Bacon and Mashed Potato	*78*
Lamb Steak Bonne Femme	*79*
Lambs' Kidneys	*81*
Lamb Steak Boulangère	*81*
Shepherd's Pie	*82*
Moussaka	*84*
Lamb Mince	*84*
Lamb Noisettes à l'Italienne	*85*

PORK

Pork Bonne Femme	*87*
Pork Goulash	*88*
Frankfurters, Sauerkraut and Mashed Potato	*88*
Pork Sausages, Red Cabbage and Apple	*89*
Garlic Sausage and Haricot Beans	*89*
Ham à la Milanaise	*91*
Warm Pork Salad	*91*
Asian Pork	*92*
Pork Fillet and Vegetables	*92*
Pork and Apple with Linguine	*93*
Smoked Pork Sausage and Flageolet Beans	*93*

VEGETARIAN AND RISOTTOS

Ratatouille and Eggs	*96*
Courgettes and Cheese Sauce	*98*
Vegetable Curry	*98*
Watercress mélange	*99*
Cauliflower Cheese	*99*
Risottos	*101*

STOCK, SAUCES AND WINE

Stock	*103*
Sauces, Mayonnaise and Vinaigrette	*103*
Béchamel Sauce	*103*
Espagnole Sauce	*104*
Cheese Sauce	*104*
Tomato Sauce	*104*
Mushroom Sauce	*105*
Sauce Vinaigrette	*105*
Mayonnaise	*106*
Wine	*106*

INTRODUCTION

As the title suggests, this book was originally written for men, but it is, of course, equally suitable for anyone cooking for themselves, or for their families. The recipes are not complicated and include quite a lot of short cuts, which some cookbook writers might not approve of! In general, the cooking times can be quite quick, although some time needs to be spent preparing the ingredients. Indeed, many writers claim short cooking times when actually much more time is spent deciding what to cook, obtaining the ingredients, doing the 'prep' before cooking and washing up afterwards!

Most of the recipes are for one main meal, but sometimes it is difficult to cut down on the ingredients and, in such cases, there may be enough for two servings. Hence you will see on some recipes "for 1 or 2." Likewise, you can double up on the ingredients if you are cooking for family or guests.

The recipes are shown in sections, including starters, soups, salads, eggs and cheese, fish, pasta, chicken, beef, lamb, pork, vegetarian and risottos. There are also brief recipes for sauces and dressings.

I have included a few starters, some of which can be used as light meals, or as a first course. However, there are no dessert recipes. If you are entertaining and need a dessert, you can always offer fruit and ice-cream, biscuits and cheese, or, better still, ask the guest to bring one along!

You will see wine used in quite a few recipes. I seldom use a traditional roux with flour, butter and milk in sauces, but often use cornflour and wine, which is lighter and quicker. (See also Sauces and Wine, Section 12)

Note that quantities are shown in ounces or fluid ounces, but there is a table on at the end which shows gram or litre equivalents.

Please don't forget to set the table and warm the plates BEFORE finishing cooking and not when you are just ready to serve!

Finally, don't get fixated by the ingredients shown in the recipes, which may not be available. Just experiment. That is all part of the learning process.

KITCHEN EQUIPMENT USED IN THESE RECIPES

Over time I have collected bits of equipment which clutter up the kitchen. I have written down below those I have used for these recipes, and it does seem rather a lot. I am reminded that, when I was a student, I got by with two mugs, three pans, a toaster, a can opener, a cork screw and a glass. Whoever heard of a student using a mortar and pestle!

However, most of these items are essential. Firstly a fridge and a cooker. If you are starting from scratch and/or space is at a premium, you can get a small combination microwave with an oven and grill. Or if you don't want a big cooker, you can get a perfectly effective micro-oven with two hot plates. An ordinary microwave is very useful for vegetables and casserole dishes, and the simplest 7 to 9 kilowatt microwave is surprisingly cheap to buy. As for food processors, these can take up a lot of room and need extra washing up. If you only want to mix or whisk, you can get a simple electric hand mixer, and if you need to mince, you could use a table hand mincer.

The other items I use are:

Toaster
Grill pan
Solid based non-stick sauté pan
Small non-stick frying pan
Non-stick wok
Set of Saucepans (including one small pan)
2 colanders
1 or 2 Pyrex casserole dishes with lids, for oven and microwave
1 or 2 plastic bowls with tops for microwave
Mixing bowl and chopping board
Weighing machine showing ounces and grams

ONE MAN COOKING

Timer, which gives a ring when time is up
Jug showing fluid ounces
Small loaf tin and baking tray

Also a bottle opener, can opener, a good potato peeler, masher, whisk, kitchen scissors, grater, tongs, wooden stirrers, large serving spoons, spatula, good cutting knives with a knife sharpener, cutlery, plates, dishes and glasses as needed, and lastly - a mortar and pestle for crushing spices!

STORE CUPBOARD INGREDIENTS USED IN THESE RECIPES

Balsamic vinegar
Basil
Bay leaves
Breadcrumbs
Capers
Cayenne Pepper
Cloves
Coriander
Cornflour
Cranberry sauce
Cream of coconut
Cumin
Curry paste
Dijon mustard
Fennel
Fish sauce
Garlic
Ginger
Juniper berries

Knorr Stockpots (chicken, fish, beef and vegetable)
Lemon juice
Mint sauce
Olive oil
Paellero (saffron type)
Peppercorns
Plain flour
Rice (long grain and risotto)
Salt
Soy sauce
Sugar
Tabasco
Thyme
Tomato purée
Turmeric
White wine
White wine vinegar

Plus Aluminium foil, Cling film and Kitchen rolls.

MICROWAVE COOKING TIMES FOR SELECTED VEGETABLES

These times are approximate, based on 700 W microwave powered on High.

For frozen vegetables, check with instructions on the pack. With dry vegetables, add two tablespoons of water. After microwaving, allow three minutes standing time, as the food goes on cooking after the oven is switched off. Don't forget to drain any vegetables after cooking.

The times are based on 4 oz portions unless stated. You need to allow extra time, if portion sizes are increased. As a general guide, increase times by a half if you double up the weight of the ingredients. If you are not satisfied that any dish is properly cooked, put it back and add extra minutes, either on High or Medium.

Minutes on High

Broad beans, fresh	5	
Broad beans, frozen	5	check pack
Runner beans, fresh	5	
Runner beans, frozen	5	check pack
Broccoli, fresh	4	
Broccoli, frozen	4	check pack
Carrots, thin	5	
Cauliflower	3	
Celery	4	
Courgettes	3	
Peas, fresh	3	
Peas, frozen	3	check pack
Spinach, fresh	3	
Spinach, frozen	3	check pack
Potatoes (4 oz)	5	

Potatoes (8 oz whole)	6
Potatoes (8 oz diced)	5

Note: some of the recipes in this book use the microwave for cooking potato. Where an extra vegetable is suggested, you can add this to the potato and increase cooking time.

1. SIMPLE STARTERS AND PÂTÉS

You may or may not want a starter if you are on your own and also cooking a main course, but you might like to provide one for family or guests. Starters range from very simple appetisers which need no cooking, to soups, hors d'oeuvres, pâtés and salads. So let's begin with the simplest starters and two of the easiest pâtés to prepare.

Asparagus
Cook for about 10 minutes in boiling water, check they are tender, but not soft, and add butter.

Avocado vinaigrette
Cut in half, remove pip and add vinaigrette (see Sauces, Section 12). Ripeness is always a problem as most shops sell avocados under-ripe. I suggest putting them in an airing cupboard, checking daily until they are ripe. Cooked prawns may be added.

Serve with brown bread and butter, cut diagonally with crust removed.

Crudités
A variety of vegetables, cut, sliced or shredded can be used and dipped into hummus, taramasalata or mayonnaise - such as celery, carrots, peppers, French beans and cauliflower florets. You can also add tomatoes, beans and cucumber slices.

Egg Mayonnaise
Hard boil one or two eggs, de-shell, halve, add mayonnaise, finally top with anchovies and milled pepper.

Hors d'oeuvres

This is a big subject in its own right, as you can choose any mixture of fish, seafood, ham, cheese, sausage, eggs and vegetables. Presentation is important. Probably the most common ingredients are sardines, sliced sausage, prawns, diced red pepper, artichoke hearts, diced cold potato, feta cheese, tomatoes, sliced cucumber, olives, beans, radishes, baby onions and asparagus tips. Add a vinaigrette dressing (see Sauces, Section 12) or a touch of mayonnaise.

Lumpfish Caviar

Real caviar would be much nicer, but this will make do, with thin brown toast.

Melon

Try Charentais, Canteloupe or Honeydew Melon. However there is the same problem in buying melons as with avocados. Shops usually sell them under-ripe. Try the airing cupboard to ripen. Press the opposite end to the stalk to test ripeness. It should give a bit and also give out a nice scent.

Parma Ham

Cut very thin and roll round cold cooked asparagus.

Pâtés (see below)

Potted Shrimps

Jars with shrimps in solid butter and spices. Good with brown toast, cut diagonally with even more butter and slices of lemon.

Prawn Cocktail

Cooked prawns set on a bed of shredded lettuce in individual glass dishes, added with mayonnaise and lemon slices. For each teaspoon of mayonnaise, mix in half a teaspoon of lemon juice, salt and milled pepper.

Rollmops

Soused herring, filleted, matured in a marinade and rolled around sliced onion. Easier to buy than make yourself. Serve with thinly sliced and diagonally quartered brown bread and butter.

Quails Eggs

Cooked and shelled. Add celery salt. Serve with thinly sliced and diagonally quartered brown bread and butter.

Salads (see Section 3)

Smoked Cod's Roe

Skinned, mashed with lemon juice and a little olive oil. Serve with toast or brown bread and butter.

Smoked Mackerel

Add lemon slices.

Smoked Salmon

Garnish with dill, milled pepper and lemon slices. Serve with brown bread and butter, or make up into tiny sandwiches with cream cheese.

Whitebait

Fresh whitebait are sometimes hard to get hold of. If you buy frozen, defrost them then dust with flour and fry in sunflower oil.

TWO SIMPLE PÂTÉS

Smoked Mackerel Pâté

    1 smoked mackerel
    1 tbsp single cream
    1 oz butter
    1 dstsp lemon juice
    Milled pepper and Cayenne pepper

Skin and de-bone mackerel. Add other ingredients and mash. Serve with brown toast.

Chicken Liver Pâté

    8 oz chicken liver
    1 oz butter
    1 clove garlic, finely chopped
    Salt, milled pepper, 1/4 tsp basil, 1/4 tsp thyme, and cayenne pepper
    1 fl oz brandy

Sauté liver briefly in half the butter. Add remaining butter and other ingredients, then blend until smooth. Put into dish or terrine and chill.

Serve with toast.

2. SOUPS

Obviously you can buy tinned soup, but it is more fun - and hopefully more tasty - to make your own. Here are half a dozen recipes for you to try, or you can make up your own ingredients and possibly use up some leftovers.

Haddock Chowder

    1 oz butter
    1 skinned fillet smoked haddock, finely chopped
    1 small onion, finely chopped
    2 stalks celery, thinly sliced
    8 oz potato, peeled and diced
    1 bay leaf
    1/2 tsp cornflour
    Milled pepper
    6 fl. oz water and milk (say 3 ozs of each)
    1 tbsp single cream

Microwave celery and potato for 5 minutes on High, and drain.
Gently fry onions in butter in a small pan. Add all ingredients to pan, except the cream. Simmer for 10-15 minutes.
Add cream, stir and serve.

Bacon and Vegetable Soup

1/2 oz butter
2 rashers bacon, sliced
1 small onion, finely chopped
1 carrot, finely chopped or grated
1 stalk celery, sliced
8 oz potato (peeled or not), diced
4 baby tomatoes, cut in half
Any left-over vegetables, chopped up
6 oz water
Salt, milled pepper and cayenne pepper

Gently fry onion and bacon in butter, in a small saucepan. Add all other ingredients and simmer for 20 minutes.

Lentil and Potato Soup

1/2 oz butter
4 oz lentils (rinsed and strained)
1 onion, finely chopped
1 stalk celery, sliced
1 carrot, finely chopped or grated
8 oz potato (peeled or not) and diced
2 rashers bacon, cut into small pieces
Milled pepper, 1/4 tsp cayenne pepper and 1/4 tsp turmeric
1/2 vegetable Stockpot
1 1/2 pints of water

Fry bacon and onion in half the butter, in a small pan. Add the remaining butter and the rest of the ingredients. Bring to the boil and simmer for 20 minutes.

ONE MAN COOKING

Bacon and Vegetable Soup

Spinach, Pea and Stilton Soup

1 oz butter
3 oz fresh (or frozen) chopped spinach
3 oz peas
3 oz Stilton, diced
4 oz milk
8 oz potato, peeled and diced
Salt, milled pepper, cayenne pepper
1/2 tsp cornflour

Microwave potato, peas and spinach for 5 minutes on High, and drain. Mix cornflour in milk and tip into a saucepan with all the ingredients. Simmer for 3-4 minutes and serve.

Lobster Chowder

1/2 oz butter
1 tin lobster bisque
1 small onion, finely chopped
8 oz potato, peeled and diced
2 rashers lean bacon, cut into small pieces
2 tbsp cream
1/2 tsp cornflour
Salt and milled pepper

Microwave potato for 5 minutes on High, and drain.

Gently fry onion and bacon in small saucepan. Add lobster bisque, potato, cream, cornflour, salt and pepper, stir.

Leave to simmer for 3-4 minutes, then serve.

Note: A drop of brandy goes well in lobster bisque!

Lobster Chowder

3. SALADS

When I wrote down the list of possible ingredients which I could think of for a salad, I was amazed. It just shows how lazy one can get by sticking to two or three favourites. There are probably several other ingredients you can add.

SALAD OPTIONS

Main Ingredients　　　　　　　　Vegetables and other

Main Ingredients		Vegetables and other
Bacon	Anchovies	Haricot beans
Chicken	Artichoke Hearts	Lentils
Crab	Asparagus	Lettuce
Eggs	Aubergines	Mushrooms
Ham	Avocados	Petit pois
Kippers	Baby sweetcorn	Potatoes
Pâtés	Bean sprouts	Red cabbage
Pork slices	Beetroot	Red onions
Prawns	Broad beans	Red/green pepper
Rare Beef	Broccoli florets	Rice
Salami slices	Cauliflower florets	Rocket
Salmon	Chicory	Snap peas
Sardines	Chives	Spinach leaves
Sausages	Courgettes	Spring Onions
Scallops	Cucumber	Tomatoes
Smoked fish	Fennel	Watercress

| Tuna | French beans |
| Turkey | |

Here follow three salads which you can try: Egg Salad, Greek Salad and *Salade Niçoise*.

Egg Salad

1 lettuce
2 hard-boiled eggs, cut in half
4 anchovy fillets
4 tomatoes, cut into quarters
Slices of cucumber
Thin slices of fennel
Vinaigrette dressing

Mix lettuce leaves, tomatoes, cucumber and fennel with vinaigrette. Place half eggs on top and anchovies on top of the eggs.

Greek Salad

1 lettuce
1 green pepper, chopped
Slices of cucumber
4 tomatoes, cut into quarters
6 black olives
4 oz feta cheese, diced
Vinaigrette dressing

Toss lettuce leaves and the other ingredients into a bowl with plenty of vinaigrette dressing.

Salade Niçoise - enough for 1 or 2

    1 tin tuna steak
    1 lettuce
    3 oz French Beans, remove ends and cut in half
    2 hard-boiled eggs, cut in half
    6 anchovy fillets
    6 black olives
    2 small potatoes, cut into quarters
    4 tomatoes, cut into quarters
    10 capers
    Several slices of cucumber
    Vinaigrette dressing (see Sauces, Section 12)

Microwave potatoes and French beans (if fresh) for 4 minutes on High, and drain.

Put lettuce leaves, tuna, French beans, olives, potatoes, tomatoes, cucumber and capers into a bowl. Add vinaigrette and mix.

Place half eggs on top, and then place anchovies on top of the eggs.

Salade Niçoise

4. EGGS AND CHEESE

Eggs in general

If you look into Montagne's unsurpassed encyclopaedia of food, wine and cooking, entitled *Larousse Gastronomique*, which was once regarded as the chef's bible, you will find nearly three hundred recipes for eggs. And that is without counting omelettes!

Here are only a few simple dishes, easy and quick to prepare, but you can always look up *Larousse*!

Scrambled Eggs and Smoked Salmon

2 eggs
2-3 oz smoked salmon, thinly sliced
1 tsp milk
1 knob of butter
Salt and milled pepper

Lightly beat eggs, milk and seasoning in a jug.
Heat small saucepan, add butter and stir in egg mixture. Keep stirring. When eggs start to solidify, stir in smoked salmon pieces.
Whilst still moist, serve immediately with buttered toast.

Omelettes

    1 knob of butter
    2 eggs
    Grated cheese, ham or sliced mushrooms
    1 tsp milk
    Salt and milled pepper

Lightly beat eggs, milk and seasoning in a jug.

Heat sauté pan, add butter, then add egg mixture. As soon as egg has started to solidify, tip in cheese, ham or mushrooms and immediately fold over with a spatula, and fold again.

The omelette should remain soft inside and firm outside, taking not more than two minutes to cook.

Serve with sauté potatoes or thin oven chips.

Omelette aux Fine Herbes

Cook as above, without ham, cheese or mushrooms, but adding chopped herbs such as basil and parsley, or tarragon and parsley.

Cheese Soufflé

    1 oz butter
    1 tbsp flour
    2 eggs
    3 oz mature cheddar cheese, grated
    6 fl oz milk
    Salt, milled pepper and paprika (or cayenne pepper)

Turn oven to 180°C.

Grease heatproof bowl with a spot of butter to stop soufflé sticking to the side.

Separate egg yolks and whites, yolks in a cup, whites in a bowl.

In a small saucepan, melt the butter, stir in the flour, add the milk, stir again, add the egg yolks, cheese and seasoning, and keep stirring on a low heat until sauce is smooth.

Pour the cheese sauce into the bowl. Whisk the egg whites until it stiffens, fold it gently into the cheese mixture.

Put the bowl into the oven for 25 minutes, or until the top turns brown.

Tortilla (Spanish Omelette)

1/2 oz butter
2 eggs
6 oz potato, peeled and diced
1 baby onion, finely chopped
1 clove garlic, finely chopped
1 tbsp milk
1/4 tsp cayenne pepper, salt and milled pepper

Microwave diced potato for 5 minutes on High, and drain.

Mix potato, eggs, milk, salt, pepper and cayenne pepper in a jug. Fry onion and garlic in butter, in small frying pan. Add egg and potato mix and fry until omelette base is firm.

With a spatula, flip omelette onto the other side and continue cooking until both sides are firm, but the inside is still moist.

Serve with salad.

Oeufs Florentine

1 knob of butter
3 oz chopped fresh spinach (5 oz if frozen)
2 slices brown bread
2 eggs
1 oz grated mature cheddar cheese
Salt and milled pepper

Cook or microwave fresh or frozen spinach for 3 minutes, and drain.

Toast 2 slices of brown bread and butter them. Place slices on grill pan or baking tray and spread spinach over each slice. Make a hollow in the spinach on each slice of bread. Crack an egg onto each hollow, add seasoning and top with cheese.

Grill until cheese goes brown when eggs should have cooked underneath.

Note: Lots of other recipes in the book use cheese, but are not singled out in this section.

Tortilla (Spanish Omelette)

5. FISH

Grilled and Sautéed Fish

Sadly the range and availability of fish around British shores has been depleted, as has been the number of decent local fishmongers. Nonetheless, there is still a range of fish available, which you can quickly sauté or grill, add a little butter and serve with vegetables of your choice.

Whole fish should be painted with olive oil and scored diagonally on both sides. White fish can be grilled or sautéed with a little butter or olive oil and needs basting. The fish should not be allowed to dry up.

Cod, coley, sole, whiting, monkfish, haddock, plaice, sea bass, halibut, herring, trout and mackerel ought to be available. Salmon cutlets, a real staple, are nearly always available but turbot is more difficult to get. Dover sole, too, is marvellous if you can get it, the bigger the better, but it is expensive. Skate cannot be grilled, but when dipped in flour, it can be sautéed in butter and served with capers and lemon juice. Likewise, whitebait, which are tiny herrings, should be dipped in flour and sautéed in butter.

If you buy fish from a supermarket or fishmonger, it should be gutted and/or filleted, but check whether you want it skinned too. If you are grilling fish, it pays to line the pan with foil first. If the fish still has its skin on, grill skin uppermost first then turn over. Baste with a little butter or olive oil and take care not to let it burn or dry out. If you are poaching fish, it is best to do this in white wine and butter or oil.

Of the shellfish, prawns and scallops should be cooked gently or they go hard. Mussels which are wide open when bought and don't close when tapped should be thrown away. Once cooked, throw away those that haven't opened.

Kedgeree

    1 oz butter
    1 skinned fillet of smoked haddock, chopped
    2 hard-boiled eggs, chopped
    1 dessert spoon curry paste
    3 oz long grain rice

Cook long grain rice for 10 minutes until nearly soft, drain, pour on boiling water and cook for another 2 minutes, then drain again. This takes out most of the starch, stops it sticking together and helps weight-watchers too!

Gently fry haddock in butter. Add curry paste and a little water, stirring occasionally, for a few minutes. Add cooked rice, and chopped egg.

Stir for 2-3 minutes and serve.

Sole Meunière

    1 oz butter
    1 or 2 fillets Dover Sole
    4 sliced mushrooms
    1 tsp capers
    1 tsp lemon juice
    4 tbsp white wine
    Salt and milled pepper
    Flour on a plate

Fry mushrooms in butter on one side of the sauté pan.

Coat sole fillets with flour on both sides and place them onto the other side of the pan. Sauté sole fillets for 2 minutes either side, then add lemon juice, capers and seasoning.

Add white wine, stir and serve with new potatoes and French Beans.

Sole Meunière

Sole Mornay

1 oz butter
1 or 2 fillets Dover Sole (or other white fish)
2 oz mature cheddar cheese, grated
2 fl oz milk
1/2 tsp cornflour
Salt, milled pepper and cayenne pepper

Mix grated cheese, milk, 1/2 oz butter and seasoning in a small pan and simmer until sauce thickens.

Grill fish fillets for 1-2 minutes each side according to thickness, basting with rest of butter.

Serve with the cheese sauce, as well as new or sauté potatoes and spinach.

Lobster Bisque Mélange

1 tbsp olive oil
1 tin lobster bisque soup
6 oz prawns
8 oz potato, peeled and diced
3 oz petit pois
4 baby tomatoes, cut in half
4 mushrooms, sliced
Salt and milled pepper

Microwave diced potato and peas for 5 minutes on High, and drain.

Gently fry prawns and mushrooms in olive oil, in a small pan, until prawns go pink (if frozen). Add tomatoes, peas, potatoes and tin of lobster bisque.

Season, stir, simmer for 2-3 minutes and serve.

Fish Casserole - for 1 or 2

1 oz butter
8 oz mixed fish pieces
4 oz cooked prawns
1 hard-boiled egg, cut into pieces
8 oz potato, peeled and diced
1 chilli pepper, finely chopped
4 baby tomatoes, cut in half
1 glass dry white wine
1 tsp cornflour
Milled pepper

Microwave diced potato for 5 minutes on High, and drain.
Stir-fry fish, prawns, chilli pepper in butter, in a small pan. Add tomatoes, egg, diced potato, white wine, cornflour and pepper.
Stir and simmer for 5 minutes.
Serve with green vegetables.

Light Tuna Curry - for 1 or 2

1 tbsp olive oil
1 tin of tuna
6 tiger prawns
1 tbsp curry paste
1 tsp sugar
4 small tomatoes, cut in half
1/4 tsp chilli powder
2 tbsp water
2 tbsp yoghurt
1 oz cream of coconut, shredded

Stir-fry prawns, tomatoes, chilli power and olive oil, in a small pan. Add the rest of the ingredients, stir, heat to simmer for a few minutes and serve with long grain rice and spinach.

Fish Casserole

Flaked Cod in Cheese Sauce

1 oz butter
8-10 oz cod, on its skin
4 oz mature cheddar, grated (for a stronger cheese flavour, try including a little blue cheese in the mix)
3 fl oz milk
1 tsp cornflour
Salt and milled papper
1/2 tsp cayenne pepper

Grill cod, first skin uppermost, turn over and grill the other side. Flake fish off the skin.

Separately, melt butter in a small pan, add cheese, milk, cornflour and seasoning. Heat and stir to a smooth sauce.

Stir in cod flakes.

To brown the sauce you can put the sauce pan (but not the handle) under the grill for 2-3 minutes.

Serve with long grain rice and vegetables of your choice.

Battered Haddock and Chips

1 tbsp of Sunflower oil
1/2 oz butter
8-10 oz skinned, smoked haddock fillet
1 white of egg
1 tbsp flour
2 tbsp tepid water
Frozen French fries

To make the batter, mix flour with 1 tbsp of sunflower oil, dilute with water, then mix until smooth. Whisk white of egg in another bowl and fold into the flour mix.

Dip the haddock into the flour mix and sauté in a pan with a little butter until cooked on both sides.

Meanwhile, put the French fries onto a grill pan, spread out and grill

for the time shown on the packet.
Serve with the haddock.

Bouillabaisse - for 2

Marseille is famous for this dish, and can include a wide variety of fish. In Marseille they sometimes add potatoes, but in Paris they add mussels.

- 2 tbsp olive oil
- 1 lb mixed white fish, chopped into pieces
- 4 oz large prawns
- 4 oz scallops
- Small onion, finely chopped
- 1 clove garlic, finely chopped
- 8 baby tomatoes, cut in half
- 2 x 4 oz glasses dry white wine
- 1/2 fish stockpot
- 1 tsp cornflour
- Salt, thyme, bay leaf and milled pepper

Stir-fry onion, garlic and all the fish with 1 tbsp of olive oil, in a saucepan. Add the second tbsp of oil and all the other ingredients. Bring to the boil and simmer for 10 minutes.

Serve with crusty bread or toast.

Smoked Haddock and Egg Mornay

- 1/2 oz butter
- 8 oz skinned, smoked haddock fillet
- 2-3 oz mature cheddar cheese, grated
- 1 egg
- 4 tbsp milk
- Milled pepper, salt and 1/2 tsp cayenne pepper
- 1 tsp cornflour

Heat butter in a small pan, add cheese, milk, cornflour and seasoning, and stir until smooth. Line a grill pan or baking tray with aluminium foil, place haddock on it, and grill and turn for 5 minutes.

Crack egg carefully over grilled haddock, pour cheese sauce on top and grill for a few more minutes until sauce goes brown.

Serve with mashed potatoes or salad.

Tuna Wok - for 1 or 2

1 tbsp olive oil
1 tin of tuna, drained
1 red pepper, chopped in pieces
2 stalks of celery, finely chopped
1 courgette, thinly sliced
6 baby tomatoes, cut in half
4 mushrooms, sliced
1 inch slice of ginger, skinned and finely chopped
1 tsp cumin, salt and milled pepper
1 glass of dry white wine

Stir-fry red pepper, celery and courgette in oil, in a wok, for about 5 minutes. Add the rest of the ingredients, stir and simmer for another few minutes.

Serve with long grain rice.

Bouillabaisse

Prawns and Spaghetti

1 tbsp olive oil
8 oz large cooked prawns
1 chilli pepper, finely chopped
1 clove garlic, finely chopped
1 small onion, finely chopped
4 oz mushrooms, sliced
6 baby tomatoes, cut in half
1 tsp cornflour, salt, milled pepper and cayenne pepper
1 glass of dry white wine
4 oz spaghetti

Stir-fry onion, garlic and chilli pepper in olive oil. Add mushrooms, tomatoes and prawns and stir.

In 3-4 minutes, add cornflour, seasoning and white wine. Stir and simmer for 5 minutes.

Meanwhile, cook spaghetti in a pan of boiling water for 10-12 minutes, and drain.

Add prawn sauce, and serve with spinach or other green vegetables.

Prawns and Spaghetti

Spanish Paella - for 1 or 2

1 tbsp olive oil
4 oz risotto rice
4 oz large cooked prawns
3 oz scallops, chopped
3 oz smoked pork sausages, chopped in pieces
3 oz *petits pois*
1/2 fish stockpot
1 little packet of flavouring called "Paellero" (or 1/2 tsp turmeric)
Milled pepper
8 fl oz water

You can also add pieces of leftover chicken, or other fish, to complement this dish

Put all ingredients into a saucepan, bring to the boil, stir occasionally, and simmer for about 16 minutes. Only add more water if needed.

Asian Prawns (hot)

1 oz butter
3 oz cooked prawns
4 mushrooms, sliced
4 baby tomatoes, cut in half
1 chilli pepper, finely chopped
2 shoots of lemongrass, finely chopped
1 small onion (or spring onion) finely chopped
Juice of 1 lime (or 1 tbsp lime juice)
1 dstsp fish sauce
1 glass dry white wine
1 tsp cornflour
1/2 tsp coriander
Salt and milled pepper

Stir-fry onion, chilli pepper and lemongrass in butter, in a wok. Add prawns, mushrooms, tomatoes, lime juice, fish sauce, coriander and seasoning. Stir-fry for about 5 minutes. Finally, add white wine and cornflour, stir until sauce thickens, and serve with long grain rice.

Scallops, Ham and Beans

1 tbsp olive oil
6 oz scallops
4 oz ham, chopped in pieces
6 oz beans (broad or flagioli)
1 glass of dry white wine
1 tsp cornflour
1 tsp sugar
Salt, milled pepper and cayenne pepper

Microwave broad beans (fresh or frozen) for 5 minutes on High, and drain.
Stir-fry scallops in olive oil. Stir in ham, beans, sugar and seasoning. Stir in cornflour and white wine.
Simmer for another 2-3 minutes, until sauce thickens.
Serve with pasta.

Fish Marsala

1 tbsp olive oil
6-8 oz white fish, cut into pieces
1 small onion, finely chopped
1 chilli pepper, finely chopped
6 oz tomatoes, chopped into quarters
1 tsp honey
1 tsp lemon juice
1 tsp cumin
1 tsp cardamom seeds
1 dstsp fish sauce

Crush cardamom seeds in a mortar and pestle. Throw away most of the outer skins.

Gently stir-fry onion, chilli pepper and cardamom in a wok in olive oil. Add all other ingredients and simmer gently for a few minutes.

Serve with long grain rice.

Moules Marinière

1 oz butter
1 - 2 lbs mussels
1 shallot, finely chopped
1 stick celery, finely chopped
1 clove garlic, finely chopped
1 tsp cornflour
Milled pepper
Parsley, finely chopped
6 oz dry white wine
1 tbsp cream

Wash mussels twice in cold water and scrape off any beards. *Throw away any open mussels that do not close when tapped.*

Put half the butter, shallots and garlic in a large saucepan and stir-fry for 2 minutes.

Put all other ingredients, except the cream, in the pan. Cover, bring to the boil and cook for 5 minutes, stirring from time to time.

Throw out any mussels that have *not* opened, and remove the half shell on the rest. The French don't usually bother to remove the half shell on each mussel, but this does look better if you have guests. Add the cream, stir and serve with French fries.

Fish Marsala

6. PASTA AND PIZZAS

There is a whole variety of pasta which can be used in these dishes. I have mostly used linguine, which is quicker to cook, as a pasta base but you can choose any number of other pastas.

Fresh pasta is sometimes available in the supermarkets. It cooks more quickly than dried pasta. Pasta is such a forgiving base in cooking that you can play around with the ingredients without going far wrong.

For dried pasta, check cooking times on the packet. Linguine, for example, is sometimes produced like spaghetti, which takes longer to cook.

Linguine in Pasta Sauce - for 1 or 2

- 1 oz butter
- 8 oz pasta sauce
- 4 oz linguine (8 oz for 2 people)
- 4 rashers lean smoked bacon, cut into slices
- 6 oz mushrooms, sliced
- 1 tiny tin of anchovies, drained and finely chopped
- 1 clove garlic
- 1 onion, finely chopped
- 1 tsp basil
- Milled pepper (no salt)

Stir-fry onion, garlic and bacon in half the butter. Add mushrooms and the rest of butter and cook for 2-3 minutes. Add anchovies, basil, pepper and pasta sauce for a further 2-3 minutes, stirring occasionally.

Meanwhile, cook linguine in a pan of salted boiling water for 7 - 9 minutes (4 if fresh).

Drain, stir in pasta sauce and serve with spinach.

Linguine alla Carbonara

1 oz butter
4 oz linguine
1 small onion, finely chopped
1 clove garlic, finely chopped
4 rashers of bacon, chopped in pieces
1 oz grated mature cheddar cheese (or parmesan)
1 egg
1 tbsp single cream
Salt and milled pepper

Stir-fry onion, bacon and garlic in butter. Add cheese, cream and seasoning. Stir until cheese melts into a sauce.

Separately, cook linguine in a pan of salted boiling water for 7 - 9 minutes (4 minutes if fresh). Drain, then add bacon and cheese sauce. Stir.

Finally, add the egg, stir and serve.

Spaghetti Bolognese

1/2 oz butter
8 oz lean beef mince
1 baby onion, finely chopped
1 clove garlic, finely chopped
1 baby carrot, finely chopped
1 stalk celery, finely chopped
3 mushrooms, sliced
1-2 oz grated mature cheddar (or parmesan) cheese
1 small tin tomatoes
1 glass dry white wine
1 tsp cornflour
Salt, milled pepper, cayenne pepper and cumin
4 oz dried spaghetti

Stir-fry onion, garlic, carrot and celery in butter, in a wok, for a few minutes. Stir in beef mince, cover wok and cook for 2-3 minutes. Add mushrooms and tinned tomatoes, and simmer for 5 minutes. Finally add seasoning, cornflour and wine, and simmer for 10-15 minutes.

Meanwhile, cook spaghetti in a pan of salted boiling water for 12 minutes. Strain, serve and sprinkle cheese on top.

Linguine, Cheese and Eggs

1 oz butter
4 oz linguine
2 hard-boiled eggs, cut into quarters
6 oz mature cheddar, grated
1 tbsp flour
5 fl oz milk
Salt and milled pepper

Melt butter in small pan, stir in flour, add milk, stir again. Add cheese and seasoning, stir on a low heat until sauce is smooth. Simmer for 2-3 minutes, then add the eggs.

Meanwhile, cook linguine in a pan of salted boiling water for 7 minutes (4 minutes if fresh). Drain, then and add cheese and egg sauce.

Linguine alla Carbonara

Linguine, Cheese and Eggs

Linguine with Mussels and Clams

1 oz butter
4 oz linguine
8 oz clams
8 oz mussels
1 small onion, finely chopped
1 clove garlic, finely chopped
6 baby tomatoes, cut in half
1 stick celery, finely chopped
6 oz dry white wine
2 tsp cornflour
Salt and milled pepper

Rinse clams and mussels twice, and remove any beards from mussels. Throw away open mussels which don't close when tapped.

Stir-fry garlic and onion in butter in a saucepan until soft. Stir in clams, mussels, tomatoes, celery, white wine, cornflour and seasoning. Put lid on saucepan and cook for 5 minutes.

At this point you can remove one or both of each mussel shell, or leave them in, but *do* discard any mussels which have not opened.

Separately, cook linguine in a pan of salted boiling water for 7 - 9 minutes (4 if fresh). Strain, add to mussel and clam sauce, and serve.

Macaroni Cheese

1 oz butter
4 oz macaroni
4 oz mature cheddar cheese, grated
4 rashers lean bacon, cut into pieces
4 fl oz milk
1 tsp cornflour
Salt and milled pepper

Put macaroni in a pan of salted boiling water for 10-12 minutes. Check when soft, and drain.

Meanwhile, fry bacon in a small saucepan with a small knob of butter for 3-4 minutes. Add the rest of the butter and the other ingredients. Stir until sauce thickens.

Add cooked macaroni, stir and serve.

Seafood Linguine

1 tbsp olive oil
4 oz linguine
4 oz cooked large prawns
3 oz scallops
6 baby tomatoes, cut in half
1 baby onion, finely chopped
1 clove garlic, finely chopped
1 chilli pepper, finely chopped
1 tsp cornflour
1 glass dry white wine
Milled pepper

Stir-fry garlic, chilli pepper and onion in olive oil to soften. Add prawns, scallops and tomatoes and cook for 5 minutes, then add wine, cornflour and milled pepper, stirring occasionally for another 5 minutes.

Meanwhile, cook linguine in a pan of salted boiling water, for 7 - 9 minutes (4 if fresh). Drain and serve with seafood sauce.

Pizzas

You can cook a variety of pizzas on a prepared pizza base, the best known of which is called a Margherita. The ingredients can include chopped ham, sausage, tuna, chicken slices, hard-boiled eggs, black olives, anchovies, red pepper, artichokes, onion, mushroom, courgettes, baby tomatoes, beans and other vegetables, pineapple, avocadoes and cheese (goats' cheese, cheddar, parmesan, but more commonly mozzarella).

To cook, first grease a baking tray to stop sticking. Add the pizza base and spread pasta sauce generously over the top, then add a few of the ingredients shown above, together with finely chopped garlic and seasoning. Sprinkle a little olive oil on top and add the cheese.

Heat the oven to 220°C. First check any cooking instructions on the packet of the pizza base, in case it differs from this recipe, then bake for about 12 minutes until the cheese is melted and goes brown.

7. CHICKEN

You can always roast a whole chicken for yourself, which has good flavour, but if you are on your own, it could last for days. The recipes which follow are generally for one meal, using chicken breasts. They are easy to get hold of, often packed in twos and threes, so you may have to double up, or save one for another day. Chicken thighs have more flavour, so you can use those instead, but you will have to take the meat off the bone before or after cooking. In addition, you can use cuts or leftovers from a whole or half chicken.

Thai Chicken

    2 tbsp sunflower oil
    1 skinless chicken breast, sliced
    1 chilli pepper, finely chopped
    1 tbsp fish sauce
    1 tbsp soy sauce
    1 tsp sugar
    1 tsp coriander powder
    1 oz cream of coconut
    1 clove garlic, finely chopped
    4 tbsp water

Fry chicken pieces, garlic and chilli pepper in sunflower oil, in a small pan.
Then crumble cream of coconut and add all the other ingredients.
Simmer for several minutes and serve with long grain rice.

Thai Chicken

Chicken Curry - for 1 or 2

    1 tbsp olive oil
    1 or 2 skinless chicken breasts, cut in slices
    1 onion, finely chopped
    1 clove garlic, finely chopped
    4 small tomatoes, cut in half
    1 red pepper, diced
    4 mushrooms, sliced
    3 tbsp yoghurt
    3 tbsp water
    1 heaped tbsp of curry paste, or if curry sauce is used, as indicated on the label of the jar.

Stir-fry garlic and onion in olive oil in a wok, until onion is soft. Add chicken slices, red pepper and curry paste, and cook for 3-4 minutes, turning the chicken pieces. Then add tomatoes, mushrooms, yoghurt and water. Put the top on the pan and simmer for 10 minutes.

Check liquid levels to suit taste. Add more water if necessary.

Serve with long grain rice.

Chicken, Pepper and Tomatoes

    1 tbsp olive oil
    1 skinless chicken breast, sliced
    1 yellow pepper, diced
    6 small tomatoes, cut in half
    1 tsp basil
    1 clove garlic, finely chopped
    1 tsp cornflour
    1 glass dry white wine
    Salt and milled pepper

Stir-fry chicken, pepper and garlic in olive oil in a wok, for 2-3 minutes. Add tomatoes, basil, cornflour, white wine and seasoning. Replace

Chicken in Black Bean Sauce

1/2 oz butter
1 or 2 skinless chicken breasts, cut into slices
1 chilli pepper, finely chopped
1 clove garlic, finely chopped
1 courgette, sliced
3 or 4 mushrooms, sliced
4 baby tomatoes, cut in half
1 piece of ginger, finely chopped
8 oz black beans, drained from tin
1 tbsp black bean sauce
Milled pepper
1 glass dry white wine
1 tsp cornflour

Stir-fry garlic and chicken slices in butter in a wok, for 2-3 minutes. Add all other ingredients and simmer gently with lid on for 10 minutes. Stir occasionally.

For two people add more mushrooms and tomatoes and rest of the tin of black beans, plus a little more white wine.

Serve with long grain rice.

Coq au Vin

1 oz butter
1 skinless chicken breast, sliced lengthways
2 rashers bacon, cut into pieces
3 baby onions (or shallots)
4 mushrooms, sliced
1 clove garlic, finely chopped

1 bay leaf
1 tsp thyme, salt and milled pepper
6 fl oz red wine
1 dstsp flour

Stir-fry chicken, bacon pieces and baby onions for a few minutes in half the butter in a wok. Add thyme, bay leaf, garlic, salt, pepper, flour, mushrooms and remaining butter and stir. Add the red wine and stir again for sauce to thicken.

Cover the wok and simmer for 10 minutes on a very low heat.

Check there is enough liquid in the sauce. If not, add a little more wine or water, and simmer for another few minutes.

Serve with long grain rice and vegetable of choice.

Chicken Casserole

1 oz butter
1 skinless chicken breast
1 onion, finely chopped
1 clove garlic, finely chopped
3 small potatoes, cut in half
1 red pepper, chopped
3 mushrooms, chopped
6 baby tomatoes, cut in half
1 stick celery, chopped
1 glass dry white wine
1 tsp cornflour
1 glass of water
1/2 chicken stockpot

Stir-fry chicken, onion, garlic, and red pepper, in butter. Transfer into a Pyrex dish with lid.

Add rest of ingredients and microwave for 12 minutes on High. Take out and stir at half-time.

Add green vegetables to the dish, either separately or in the microwave.

Asian Chicken

1 tbsp sunflower oil
1 skinless chicken breast, sliced
1 chilli pepper, finely chopped
1 clove garlic, finely chopped
4 baby tomatoes, cut in half
3 mushrooms, sliced
1 dstsp soy sauce
1 tsp fish sauce
1 tsp sugar
1 tsp cornflour
Salt and pepper
1 glass of dry white wine

Stir-fry chicken slices, chilli pepper and garlic in sunflower oil. Add tomatoes and mushrooms. Stir and simmer for 2 minutes. Add fish sauce, soy sauce and sugar. Stir and simmer for 2 minutes. Add cornflour, white wine and seasoning, stir to thicken for 2-3 minutes.

Serve with long grain rice and vegetables of your choice.

Chicken Valentine

1 oz butter
1 skinless chicken breast

Flatten chicken breast.

Heat sauté pan to hot and fry chicken in butter until browning on both sides. Press down occasionally in the pan with a spatula to ensure chicken is cooked through.

Serve with salad and French fries.

Chicken in Black Bean Sauce

Asian Chicken

Chicken in Pasta Sauce

2 tbsp olive oil
1 skinless chicken breast, cut into pieces
8 oz potato, peeled and diced
1 chilli pepper, finely chopped
1 red pepper, chopped
1 clove garlic, finely chopped
4 mushrooms, sliced
6 tbsp pasta sauce
1 tsp paprika, salt and milled pepper

Microwave potato for 5 minutes on High, and drain.

Stir-fry chicken, red pepper, chilli pepper and garlic in olive oil, in a wok. Add potato, mushrooms, paprika, salt and pepper. Finally, add pasta sauce, more if needed, and simmer for several minutes.

Serve with broccoli, spinach, or other green vegetable.

Chicken Paprika

1 tbsp olive oil
1 skinless chicken breast, sliced into strips and cut in half
1 tbsp paprika
1 clove garlic, finely chopped
1 tsp cornflour
1 glass of dry white wine
2 tbsp cream

Cook chicken pieces and garlic in olive oil, in small saucepan or frying pan, until turning brown. Add paprika, cornflour and wine. Stir, simmer to thicken sauce, and add cream.

Chicken Paprika

Chicken in Mushroom Sauce

1 oz butter
1 skinless chicken breast, sliced
8 mushrooms, sliced
1 piece ginger, cut into small pieces
1 dstsp flour
4 fl oz milk
1 tbsp cream
Salt, plenty of milled pepper and 1/2 tsp cayenne pepper

Put chicken pieces and butter into a small pan and fry gently. Add mushroom slices, ginger, flour, seasoning, cayenne pepper and stir. Add milk, stir and simmer for 5 minutes. Add cream, simmer and keep warm until vegetables are ready.

Serve with long grain rice and green vegetables.

Chicken Leftovers

1 oz butter
8 oz cooked chicken, cut into pieces
2 rashers lean bacon, cut into strips
6 oz mushrooms, sliced
6 oz milk
1 level dstsp flour
Salt, milled pepper, cayenne pepper

Fry bacon in butter, in small saucepan. Add mushrooms and stir. Add chicken, flour, seasoning and stir. Add milk, stir and simmer for a few minutes until it thickens.

You can add some leftover green vegetables, or cook vegetables separately.

8. BEEF

There is a range of cuts of beef, like steak or chops, which can be quickly grilled or pan-fried and served either with French fries and vegetables, or with a garnish such as *Bonne Femme*.

In general, frying beef quickly in a very hot sauté pan, either in sunflower oil, groundnut oil or butter gives a better flavour than grilling. However, some beef cuts have more flavour after one or two hours cooking. For cooking steak quickly, fillet steak is the most tender, followed by sirloin, and then by rump. If you buy sirloin or rump, it is always more tender if it has matured for three to four weeks before purchase. For cooking fillet steak rare, one minute each side in a hot sauté pan can be enough.

Steak and French Fries

1 oz butter
1 slice fillet steak or sirloin
4 mushrooms, sliced
2 tomatoes, halved
French fries

Cook steak for 2 minutes each side (sirloin) or a little over 1 minute (fillet) in half the butter, in a hot sauté pan.

Remove the steak to rest and cook the mushrooms and tomatoes in remaining butter until soft.

Meanwhile, prepare French fries under the grill or in the oven, as shown on the packet.

Steak and French Fries

Boeuf Bourguignon

1 oz butter
1 slice sirloin or fillet steak
2 rashers bacon, cut into strips
8 button mushrooms
2 small onions, finely chopped
3 button onions
1/4 tsp thyme
Milled pepper
1 glass red wine
1 glass of water
1 tsp cornflour
1 tbsp single cream

Brush steak with sunflower oil and cook in hot sauté pan for 2 minutes each side.

Remove steak from pan, rest for 5 minutes, trim off fat and cut into small pieces or thin strips.

Add bacon slices, butter and all the onions to hot sauté pan, and cook until brown. Stir in mushrooms, thyme and milled pepper and cook for about a minute, then stir in cornflour, wine, water and cream. Bring to simmer until sauce thickens.

Finally, stir in meat pieces and serve with long grain rice.

Beef Curry

Brush of sunflower oil
1 slice sirloin or fillet steak
1 onion, finely chopped
1 chilli pepper, finely chopped
4 mushrooms, sliced
6 baby tomatoes, cut in half
1 tbsp curry paste
1/4 tsp each of cumin and coriander

2 tbsp yoghurt
4 fl oz water

Brush steak with sunflower oil and cook in hot sauté pan for 2 minutes each side.

Remove steak from pan, rest for 5 minutes, trim off fat and cut into small pieces or thin strips.

Meanwhile, put all the other ingredients into covered Pyrex dish and microwave on High for 5 minutes.

Stir meat pieces into Pyrex dish and serve with long grain rice.

Minute Steak and Mashed Potato

1 oz butter
1 slice sirloin or fillet steak
4 mushrooms, sliced
4 small tomatoes, cut in half
1 large potato, peeled and diced
Salt and milled pepper
1 glass white wine
1 tsp cornflour
Little milk

Microwave diced potato on High for 6 minutes, and drain. (If you like, you can add another vegetable at the same time but allow more cooking time.) Mash diced potato pieces with a little milk, half the butter and seasoning.

Brush the steak with sunflower oil and cook in hot sauté pan for 2 minutes each side.

Remove steak, put mushrooms and tomatoes in hot sauté pan with remaining butter, and cook for 2 minutes. Add the cornflour and glass of wine. Stir and cook for another 2-3 minutes until sauce has thickened.

Replace the steak in the pan, stir and serve.

ONE MAN COOKING

Minute Steak and Mashed Potato

Beef Casserole - for 1 or 2

1/2 oz butter
1 slice sirloin or fillet steak
1 small onion, finely chopped
1 clove garlic, finely chopped
4 baby carrots, finely chopped
2 stalks celery, finely chopped
4 baby tomatoes, cut in half
4 mushrooms, sliced
8 oz potato, peeled and diced
3 oz peas or beans
1/2 beef stockpot
1 glass white wine
1 glass water
1 tsp cornflour
Salt and milled pepper

Brush steak with sunflower oil and cook in hot sauté pan for 2 minutes each side.

Remove steak from pan, rest for 5 minutes, trim off fat and cut into small pieces or thin strips.

Meanwhile, microwave all the other ingredients in a covered Pyrex dish on High for 10 minutes. Stir and microwave for another 5 minutes.

Finally, stir steak pieces in Pyrex dish and serve.

Carbonade Flamande

1/2 oz butter
Brush sunflower oil
1 slice sirloin or fillet steak
1 small onion, finely chopped
1 clove garlic, finely chopped
3 mushrooms, sliced

3 small tomatoes, cut in half
1 tsp thyme
1 tsp flour
Salt and milled pepper
4 fl oz beer

Brush steak pieces with sunflower oil and cook in hot sauté pan for 2 minutes each side.

Remove steak from pan, rest for 5 minutes, trim off fat and cut into small pieces or thin strips.

Meanwhile, put all the other ingredients into covered Pyrex dish. Stir and microwave on High for 3 minutes.

Finally stir meat pieces in Pyrex dish and serve with potatoes, mashed or otherwise, and green vegetables.

Beef Stroganoff

1 oz butter
1 slice of fillet steak, cut into thin strips
1 small onion, finely chopped
1/2 tsp curry powder or paste
1/2 beef stockpot
1 tsp tomato purée
1 tbsp soured cream
1 tsp cornflour
1 glass of white wine
1 tbsp brandy

Stir-fry onion in butter, in a wok. Add fillet strips for 2 minutes and stir, then add all other ingredients except the brandy and simmer until the sauce thickens. Finally, add the brandy, stir and serve with rice and vegetables of choice.

Beef Stroganoff

Stuffed Pepper

    1/2 oz butter
    1 red pepper, top sliced, hollowed out and rinsed
    8 oz lean beef mince
    1 small onion, finely chopped
    1 clove garlic, finely chopped
    1 stalk celery, finely chopped
    3 mushrooms, sliced
    1 tsp cumin, 1/2 tsp cayenne pepper
    Salt and milled pepper
    2 tbsp pasta sauce
    1/2 beef stockpot
    1 glass of dry white wine
    For two people, add another pepper and a little more mince.

Fry onion, garlic and butter in a small pan. Add mince and celery and stir for 2 minutes. Add mushrooms, seasoning, pasta sauce, beef stockpot and stir for 2 minutes. Add white wine, stir and simmer for 10 minutes.

Put red pepper into a covered Pyrex dish, then press all the ingredients into the red pepper with the rest round the side.

Microwave for 10 minutes on High.

Serve with long grain rice.

Boeuf Boulangère

    Sunflower oil
    1/2 oz butter
    1 slice sirloin or fillet steak
    1 small onion, finely chopped
    3 baby onions, peeled
    8 oz new or baby potatoes, cut in half
    Salt and milled pepper
    1 tsp cornflour
    1 glass of dry white wine
    1 tbsp cranberry sauce

Microwave potatoes for 5 minutes on High, and drain.

Brush steak with sunflower oil and sauté for 2 minutes each side in hot sauté pan (less for fillet steak if wanted rare). Take steak out and allow it to rest.

Stir-fry onions and baby onions in butter in the hot sauté pan. Add potatoes, cornflour, seasoning, wine and cranberry sauce to sauté pan and simmer until sauce thickens.

Replace steak in pan, stir and serve with green vegetables of choice.

Chilli con Carne - for 1 or 2

1/2 oz butter
8 oz lean beef mince
1 tin red kidney beans, drained and rinsed
1 small onion, finely chopped
1 clove garlic, finely chopped
1 chilli pepper, finely chopped
1 red pepper, cut into pieces
2 tomatoes, sliced (optional)
2 mushrooms, sliced (optional)
2 tbsp pasta sauce (optional)
1/2 tsp cumin
1/2 tsp coriander
6 fl oz water (or wine)
Milled pepper
1/2 beef stockpot

Stir-fry onion, garlic and chilli pepper in butter. Add mince, red pepper, stir and simmer for 2-3 minutes. Add beans, tomatoes, mushrooms, cumin, coriander, pepper, beef stockpot, pasta sauce, water (or wine) and stir. Simmer for another 10 minutes.

Serve with rice.

Chilli con Carne

Boeuf à la Bonne Femme - for 1 or 2

1 oz butter
1 slice sirloin or fillet steak
8 oz potato, peeled and diced
1 small onion, finely chopped
1 clove garlic, finely chopped
3 rashers bacon, sliced
3 mushrooms, sliced
3 baby tomatoes, cut in half
3 baby onions, peeled
Salt and milled pepper
1 tsp cornflour
6 ozs dry white wine

Microwave diced potato for 5 minutes on High, and drain.

Brush steak with sunflower oil and cook in a hot sauté pan for 2 minutes each side (less for fillet steak if wanted rare). Take steak out of pan and allow it to rest.

Stir-fry chopped onion, baby onions, bacon and garlic in butter in hot sauté pan. Add mushrooms, tomatoes, seasoning, cornflour, diced potato and simmer until sauce thickens.

Replace steak in pan, stir and serve with green vegetable of choice.

Steak Tartare

8 oz fillet steak, minced or finely chopped
1 egg yolk
1 tbsp capers, cut in half
1 slice of onion, finely chopped
Milled pepper

Mix steak with egg yolk, onion, capers and seasoning in a bowl and serve with salad and French fries.

Veal Stew

1 escalope of veal
8 oz potato, peeled and diced
1 small onion, finely chopped
2 carrots, finely chopped
2 stalks celery, finely chopped
2 tomatoes, cut into quarters
5 mushrooms, sliced
1 clove garlic, finely chopped
1 squeeze tomato purée
1/2 *Knorr* vegetable stockpot
Milled pepper
4 fl oz water

Microwave all ingredients, except the veal escalope, in a covered Pyrex dish on High for 15 minutes. Meanwhile, heat sauté pan to hot, brush veal escalope with sunflower oil and sauté for 2 minutes each side.

Cut veal escalope into pieces, add to Pyrex dish, stir and serve.

Steak au Poivre

1 oz butter
1 slice of fillet steak
Crushed pepper (in mortar and pestle)
1 tbsp single cream
3 tbsp red wine
1 clove garlic, finely chopped
A little salt

Crush peppercorns, brush steak with sunflower oil, press peppercorns onto steak. Heat sauté pan to hot, cook steak for 1-2 minutes either side. Remove steak onto serving plate.

Add butter, garlic, cream, salt and red wine to hot sauté pan. Stir and add to steak.

Serve with mashed potato and green vegetable of choice.

Veal Stew

Wiener Schnitzel

    1/2 oz butter
    1 escalope of veal
    1 egg
    1 oz flour
    1 dstsp water
    Golden breadcrumbs
    Seasoning

Whisk egg, water and seasoning in a bowl.

Sprinkle flour and breadcrumbs on separate plates or on a flat surface. Dip veal into flour on both sides, then into the egg mix and finally into the breadcrumbs.

Heat sauté pan to hot, cook veal in butter for 2-3 minutes on each side (depending on thickness).

Serve with oven-cooked chips or sauté potatoes and green vegetable of choice.

Corned Beef Hash - for 1 or 2

    1/2 oz butter
    1 tin of corned beef, cut into slices
    1 tin of tomatoes
    1 onion, finely chopped
    4 mushrooms, sliced
    Salt and milled pepper

Stir-fry onion in butter in a wok or sauté pan. Add corned beef and mushrooms, cook lightly and stir. Add tomatoes and seasoning, stir and simmer for 6-8 minutes.

Serve with long grain rice and green vegetable of choice.

Calves' Liver and Bacon

1 oz butter
1 slice of calves liver, about a finger thick
2 rashers bacon, cut into thin slices
1 small onion, finely chopped
4 mushrooms, cut into pieces
8 oz potato, peeled and diced
1 oz flour on a plate
1/2 tsp cornflour
1 glass of dry white or red wine
Salt and milled pepper

Microwave diced potato for 5 minutes on High, and drain.

Coat liver in flour, fry for 1-2 minutes each side in half the butter in a sauté pan. Remove liver to serving plate and keep warm.

In the hot sauté pan, fry onion and bacon, seasoning, mushrooms, potato, and the rest of the butter for a few minutes. Add cornflour and wine and stir until sauce thickens.

Serve with the liver and spinach.

Wiener Schnitzel

9. LAMB

Welsh spring lamb is said to be the best, but all English and New Zealand lamb is first-rate, whether or not with new potatoes and *petits pois*. The cuts that can be prepared quickly include lamb steaks cut from the fillet end of the leg, lamb chops cut from the loin, lamb cutlets taken from the rib, noisettes - which are deboned cutlets - not forgetting the liver and kidneys.

Lamb Curry

    8-10 oz lamb steak
    1 onion, finely chopped
    4 mushrooms, sliced
    1 chilli pepper, finely chopped
    6 baby tomatoes, cut in half
    1 tbsp curry paste
    1/4 tsp each coriander and cumin
    2 tbsp yoghurt
    4 fl oz water

Stir and microwave all the ingredients, except the lamb, for 6 minutes on High, in a covered Pyrex dish.

Meanwhile, cut lamb steak into small pieces, brush them with sunflower oil and sauté in a hot pan for 3 minutes, turning them over.

Add lamb pieces to Pyrex dish and stir, then microwave Pyrex dish on Medium for 2 minutes.

Lamb Curry

Quick Cassoulet - enough for 2

1/2 oz butter
10 oz minced lamb
10 oz haricot beans (from tin) drained
10 oz garlic sausage cut into pieces
3 rashers bacon, sliced
1 dstsp chopped rosemary
1 tsp thyme
2 dessertspoons tomato purée
8 fl oz dry white wine
Salt and milled pepper
Breadcrumbs

Stir-fry lamb, garlic sausage and bacon in butter in a small saucepan until brown. Add haricot beans, herbs, tomato purée, seasoning, white wine, and stir. Simmer with lid on for 10-15 minutes.

Add breadcrumb topping and serve with rice and green vegetable of choice.

Lamb's Liver, Bacon and Mashed Potato

1 oz butter
6-9 oz lamb's liver, thinly sliced
3 rashers of bacon, sliced
3 mushrooms, sliced
8 oz potato, peeled and diced
1 tsp cornflour
1 glass of dry white wine
Seasoning
3-4 tbsp milk

Microwave potato in covered Pyrex dish for 6 minutes on High, and drain. Mash with milk, half the butter and seasoning.

Separately, stir-fry bacon and mushrooms in the other half of butter for 3-4 minutes. Add liver and cook for 1 minute each side. Add cornflour, wine and stir. Simmer for 2-3 minutes until sauce thickens.

Serve with the mashed potato and any green vegetable of choice.

Lamb Steak Bonne Femme - for 1 or 2

1 oz butter
8-10 oz lamb leg steak
8 oz potato, peeled and diced
1 small onion, finely chopped
1 clove of garlic, finely chopped
3 rashers bacon, sliced
3 baby onions, peeled
3 mushrooms, sliced
3 baby tomatoes, cut in half
Salt and milled pepper

1 tsp cornflour
6 oz dry white wine

Microwave potato for 5 minutes on High, and drain.

Brush lamb steak with sunflower oil and cook in a hot sauté pan for 2 minutes each side. Take steak out of sauté pan and allow it to rest.

Stir-fry chopped onion, baby onions, bacon and garlic in butter in the hot sauté pan. Add mushrooms, tomatoes, seasoning, cornflour, wine and diced potato until sauce thickens.

Replace lamb steak in pan, stir and serve with green vegetable of choice.

Lamb Steak Bonne Femme

Lambs' Kidneys

1/2 oz butter
3 lambs' kidneys
2 rashers bacon, sliced
3 mushrooms, thinly sliced
3 baby tomatoes, halved
Salt and milled pepper
1 tsp cornflour
1 glass of dry white wine

Slice kidneys, lengthways, and cut or snip out the gristly cores. Stir-fry kidneys and bacon in butter in a wok. Add mushrooms, tomatoes, seasoning and stir for 2-3 minutes. Add cornflour and wine, stir and simmer until sauce thickens.

Serve with rice and vegetable of choice.

Lamb Steak Boulangère

1/2 oz butter
8 oz lamb leg steak
1 small onion, finely chopped
3 baby onions peeled
8 oz new or baby potatoes
Salt and milled pepper
1 tsp cornflour
1 glass of dry white wine
1 tbsp cranberry sauce

Microwave potatoes for 6 minutes on High, and drain.

Brush steak with sunflower oil and sauté for 2 minutes each side in hot sauté pan. Take steak out and allow it to rest.

Stir-fry onion and baby onions in butter in the hot sauté pan. Add potatoes, cornflour, seasoning, wine and cranberry sauce to sauté pan and simmer until sauce thickens.

Replace lamb steak in pan, stir and serve with green vegetable of choice.

Shepherd's Pie

1 oz butter
8 oz lamb mince
1 small onion, finely chopped
1 clove garlic, finely chopped
3 baby carrots, finely chopped
3 tomatoes, sliced
3 mushrooms, sliced
1 tsp cornflour
1/2 beef stockpot
Seasoning
2 tbsp pasta sauce
8 oz potatoes, peeled and diced
Dash of milk

Stir-fry onion, garlic, mince and carrots in half the butter, in a wok or small saucepan. Add tomatoes, mushrooms, beef stockpot and pasta sauce. Cover with lid and simmer for 10 minutes. Stir in seasoning, cornflour and simmer for another 2 minutes, then tip the ingredients into a Pyrex dish.

Meanwhile, microwave diced potato for 6 minutes on High, and drain. Mash with the other half of the butter, a little milk and seasoning and place the mash on top of the mince in the Pyrex dish. Place Pyrex dish under grill until the top of the potato goes brown.

Serve with green vegetable of choice.

Shepherd's Pie

Moussaka

1/2 oz butter
3 tbsp olive oil
8 oz minced lamb
1 small onion, finely chopped
3 slices aubergine
3 baby tomatoes
3 tbsp milk
Seasoning
3 oz grated cheese
1/2 tsp cornflour

Stir-fry onion in small pan with 1 tbsp olive oil, until soft. Add lamb, tomatoes, seasoning and a tbsp of water. Simmer for 5 minutes.

When cooked, tip ingredients into a Pyrex dish, then brush the aubergine slices with olive oil on both sides and fry in the small pan. Place the slices of aubergine on top of the mince in the Pyrex dish.

Put grated cheese, milk, butter and cornflour in the small pan, heat and stir until the sauce thickens, then spread it over the aubergines in the Pyrex dish.

Finally, put the Pyrex dish under the grill until the cheese topping goes brown.

Serve with rice and spinach.

Lamb Mince

1/2 oz butter
10 oz minced lamb
1 small onion, finely chopped
1 tin chopped tomatoes
1/2 tsp cumin
1/2 tsp coriander
1/4 tsp cayenne pepper
Salt and milled pepper

Stir-fry onion in butter in a wok or small pan until soft. Add minced lamb and simmer until it goes brown. Add tomatoes, spices, salt and pepper, then simmer for a further 5-10 minutes.

Serve with rice and green vegetable of choice.

Lamb Noisettes à l'Italienne

2 tbsp sunflower oil
2 slices white bread
4 lamb noisettes (deboned cutlets)
3 mushrooms, sliced thinly
1 slice ham cut into 2-inch squares
1 slice ham cut into fine pieces
1 tbsp tomato purée
Seasoning
1 wine glass dry white wine
Chopped parsley

This is a bit more *haute cuisine*!

First cut white bread into croutons and fry in sunflower oil in sauté pan until brown. Remove croutons onto a hot serving plate and keep warm.

Sauté lamb noisettes in the hot sauté pan for 2 minutes each side. Place the noisettes on top of the croutons on the serving plate and place the 2-inch-square ham pieces on top of each noisette.

Simmer the mushrooms, seasoning, chopped parsley and tomato purée for 3 minutes in the sauté pan. Stir in the chopped ham and spoon them on top of each noisette.

Serve with green vegetables.

Lamb Noisettes à l'Italienne

10. PORK

The pig is a very generous animal, giving us bacon, ham, gammon, liver and lots of succulent cuts. Sadly, many of the choicest cuts are too large for one or two, and need a lot of cooking. However there is one cut, fillet or tenderloin of pork, cut from the ribs, which is widely available, and if sliced, can be sautéed in minutes.

Pork Bonne Femme

1 oz butter
6-8 oz pork fillet, cut in slices
1 small onion, finely chopped
3 baby onions, peeled
1 clove garlic, finely chopped
3 rashers bacon, cut into pieces
3 mushrooms, sliced
3 baby tomatoes, cut in half
8 oz potato, peeled and diced
1 tsp cornflour
Salt and milled pepper
6 oz glass of dry white wine

Microwave diced potato for 5 minutes on High, and drain.

Meanwhile, heat sauté pan and fry pork slices with bacon, all the onion and garlic in half the butter, until they start to brown, then stir in mushrooms, tomatoes, diced potato and remaining butter. Finally, add cornflour, seasoning and wine. Stir, simmer until sauce thickens and serve with vegetable of choice.

Pork Goulash

1 dstsp sunflower oil
6-8 oz pork fillet, cut into slices
1 onion, finely chopped
1 red pepper, finely chopped
1 clove garlic, finely chopped
1 small tin of tomatoes
2 tbsp paprika
1 tsp cornflour
2 tbsp soured single cream
Salt to taste

Stir-fry onion, red pepper, garlic and pork fillet slices in sunflower oil, in a hot wok, for 3-4 minutes. Add paprika, salt, cream and tomatoes and simmer for another 3-4 minutes. Add cornflour, stir until sauce thickens, and serve.

Serve with long grain rice and green vegetable of choice.

Frankfurters, Sauerkraut and Mashed Potato

1/2 oz butter
6-8 frankfurters
6 oz sauerkraut
8 oz potato, peeled and diced
3-4 tbsp milk
Salt and milled pepper

Microwave diced potato for 6 minutes on High, and drain. Mash with butter, milk and seasoning.

Separately, simmer frankfurters for 3-4 minutes in a pan of hot water. Remove sausages to serving plate.

Heat sauerkraut in a spot of hot water for a couple of minutes. Drain sauerkraut, add to mashed potato and frankfurters.

Pork Sausages, Red Cabbage and Apple

1/2 oz butter
4 pork sausages
8 oz red cabbage, finely chopped
1 cooking apple, finely chopped
1 small onion, peeled
1 tbsp olive oil
1 tbsp white wine vinegar
1 tbsp water
1 tbsp brown sugar
6 cloves
Salt, milled pepper and a pinch of cinnamon

Grill sausages.

Meanwhile, put all other ingredients in a covered Pyrex bowl and microwave on High for 12 minutes. Stop microwave half way, stir and restart. Taste to ensure red cabbage is properly cooked. If not, restart microwave again. Finally, remove onion and stir. Serve with the sausages and mashed potato.

Garlic Sausage and Haricot Beans

1/2 oz butter
1 red pepper, diced
1 small onion, finely chopped
6-8 oz garlic sausage, cut off skin and diced
1 small tin chopped tomatoes
1 tin (or less) haricot beans, drained
1/2 chicken stockpot
Salt, milled pepper and 1 tsp cumin

Stir-fry pepper, onion and butter in a small pan. Add tomatoes, diced garlic sausage, haricot beans, chicken stockpot and seasoning. Simmer for a few minutes, and serve with broccoli or other green vegetable.

Pork Sausages, Red Cabbage and Apple

Ham à la Milanaise

1/2 oz butter
1 slice ham, pencil thick, cut in strips
1 egg, beaten
Breadcrumbs
2 tomatoes, sliced
2 oz grated cheese
Salt

Dip ham strips into bowl of beaten egg, then into breadcrumbs, then into a hot buttered sauté pan. Cook on both sides for 2 minutes, add sliced tomatoes, salt and cover with grated cheese.

Put sauté pan (not the handle) under grill, until cheese melts and starts to brown.

Serve with spinach and French fries.

Warm Pork Salad

1 small lettuce
6 oz pork fillet, cut into slices
Several slices of cucumber
6 baby tomatoes, cut in half
1/2 tin of butter beans, drained
Sauce Vinaigrette

Prepare salad of lettuce, cucumber, tomatoes and beans with vinaigrette, stir and plate.

Stir-fry pork fillet in a wok with a teaspoon of sunflower oil. When cooked on both sides, cut pork into quarters, toss into the plated salad, stir, warm for 1 minute under the grill, and serve.

Asian Pork

1/2 oz butter
6-8 oz pork fillet, cut into slices
1 small onion, finely chopped
1 clove garlic, finely chopped
6 small tomatoes, cut in half
2 tbsp white wine vinegar
1 tbsp sugar
1/2 tsp powdered chilli pepper
1/2 tsp cumin
1/2 tsp coriander
1 tsp cornflour
Salt and milled pepper
1 glass of dry white wine

Stir-fry onion in butter, in a wok. Add pork fillet slices to brown. Add garlic, sugar, vinegar, tomatoes, chilli pepper, cumin, coriander, salt, milled pepper and stir for 2 minutes. Add cornflour, wine, simmer until sauce thickens, and serve with long grain rice and green vegetables of choice.

Pork Fillet and Vegetables

1 dstsp olive oil
6-8 oz pork fillet, cut in slices
4 new potatoes, cut in half (or 8 oz potato diced)
6 baby tomatoes, cut in half
1 onion, finely sliced
1 stick celery, finely sliced
3 oz runner beans, broad beans or mange tout
Salt and milled pepper
1 tsp cornflour
1 glass of dry white wine

Microwave potatoes, celery, beans or mange tout for 8 minutes on High, and drain.

Stir-fry onion and pork slices (both sides) in olive oil in a hot wok for 3 minutes. Add potatoes, celery, beans or mange tout, tomatoes, seasoning to the wok and stir. Add wine and cornflour, stir, simmer until sauce has thickened, then serve.

Pork and Apple with Linguine

    6-8 oz pork fillet, cut into slices, then again in half
    1 large apple, peeled and chopped finely
    1 tbsp sugar
    5 cloves
    1 piece ginger, chopped finely
    1 tsp cornflour
    1 glass of dry white wine
    3 oz linguine

Brush pork slices with sunflower oil and cook to brown in a saucepan. Add apple, sugar, ginger and cloves, cover pan with lid and simmer until apple softens, then stir in cornflour and white wine, simmer until sauce thickens.

Meanwhile, cook linguine in a pan of boiling water for 7 - 9 minutes (4 if fresh). Drain, stir in pork and apple sauce, and serve.

Smoked Pork Sausage and Flageolet Beans

    1 oz butter
    3 smoked pork sausages, finely sliced
    1 tin flageolet beans, drained
    3 baby tomatoes, sliced
    3 mushrooms, sliced
    3 new or small potatoes, cut in half
    Salt and milled pepper
    2 tbsp of water

Microwave potatoes for 5 minutes on High, and drain. Put the other ingredients in a small pan and heat to simmer. Add potatoes, simmer and serve.

Ham à la Milanaise

ONE MAN COOKING

Pork Fillet and Vegetables

11. VEGETARIAN AND RISOTTOS

Ratatouille and Eggs

2-3 tbsp olive oil
2 hard-boiled eggs, cut in half
1 onion, finely chopped
1 clove garlic, finely chopped,
1 aubergine, diced
1 red pepper, skinned and diced
1 green pepper, skinned and diced
2 courgettes, thinly sliced
1 dstsp coriander
Salt and milled pepper
3 tomatoes, cut into quarters
1 small tin of chopped tomatoes

Stir-fry onion and garlic in a little olive oil in a saucepan, until soft. Add the rest of the oil and all the other ingredients, except the eggs.

Heat the pan, simmer for about 25 minutes and stir. If you want a little more juice, add a dash of white wine, then add the eggs.

Serve with either long grain rice, or new or baked potatoes.

ONE MAN COOKING

Ratatouille and Eggs

Courgettes and Cheese Sauce

1/2 oz butter
2 - 4 courgettes, sliced down the middle, lengthways
4 oz grated mature cheddar cheese
3-4 fl oz milk
Salt and milled pepper
1 tsp cornflour
1/2 tsp cayenne pepper

Brush courgette pieces with sunflower oil and place cut-side down in a grill pan or baking tray. Grill and turn until brown, both sides.

Meanwhile, mix cheese, milk, butter, seasoning and cornflour in a small pan. Cook for a few minutes until sauce thickens.

Top the courgettes with the sauce and place under the grill until cheese starts turning brown.

Serve with long grain rice.

Vegetable Curry - for 1 or 2

1 oz butter
1 onion, finely chopped
2 red pepper, finely chopped
1 chilli pepper, finely chopped
2 oz baby carrots, finely chopped
1 or 2 stalks celery, finely chopped
4 oz mushrooms, chopped
4 tomatoes, chopped
4 oz yoghurt
2 tbsp curry paste

Put onion, red pepper, chilli pepper, carrots and celery in a Pyrex bowl with cover and microwave for 10 minutes on High. Remove bowl and add mushrooms, tomatoes, yoghurt and curry paste. Stir and microwave for another 8 minutes on High.

Serve with long grain rice.

Watercress mélange

1 dstsp olive oil
1 bunch watercress, chopped up
8 oz potatoes, peeled and diced
2 hard-boiled eggs, chopped
2 oz grated mature cheese
4 fl oz water
1/2 chicken stockpot

Microwave diced potato for 5 minutes on High, and drain.

Cook chopped watercress in a small pan with 4 fl oz of boiling water for 2 minutes. Add cheese, chopped egg, potato, olive oil and 1/2 chicken stockpot to the watercress. Stir, simmer for 3-4 minutes and serve.

Cauliflower Cheese

1 oz butter
1/2 cauliflower, cut into florets
4 oz mature grated cheese
3-4 fl oz milk
Salt and milled pepper
1 tsp cornflour

Microwave cauliflower for 5-6 minutes on High (dependent on size), and drain.

Melt butter in small pan and add cheese, milk, cornflour and seasoning. Stir until sauce thickens.

Place cauliflower florets on a grill pan or baking tray, add the sauce and cook under the grill until sauce goes brown. You can also add any leftover vegetables - or sliced tomato - to the cauliflower before pouring over the cheese sauce.

Serve with long grain rice.

Cauliflower Cheese

Risottos

You can make any number of risottos with fish, beef, ham, chopped egg, vegetables, or whatever you like. The basic ingredient is Arborio rice, which you allow to thicken, instead of draining off the starch, as is recommended for long grain rice.

Some people take hours to cook a risotto, but it is not necessary. Providing you know that the rice takes about twenty minutes to cook, you can add ingredients along the way. For example, let's start with a **Chicken Risotto** with ingredients as follows:

1 oz butter
4 oz Arborio rice
12 fl oz water
6 oz cooked chicken leftovers
1 onion, finely chopped
4 oz asparagus tips
3 oz petit pois
1 oz grated parmesan cheese
Salt and milled pepper
2 fl oz white wine
1/2 chicken stockpot

Stir-fry onion in a pan with butter for 2-3 minutes. Add rice and stir for 1 minute. Add water, bring to simmer. Add *petits pois*, asparagus tips, chicken stockpot, salt and milled pepper. Wait until rice is nearly cooked then add chicken leftovers.

Test the rice 18 minutes after adding water. If cooked, stir in parmesan cheese. If not quite cooked, stir in 1 or 2 fl oz white wine, then add parmesan cheese and cook for a further minute or two.

Risottos

12. STOCK, SAUCES AND WINE

Stock

Stock, of one kind or another, forms the basis for a lot *haute cuisine* dishes. You can make your own, but it is rather time consuming. Alternatively, you can buy packaged stock from the shops, or you can use tablets, watered down, or what are called 'stockpots.' The old fashioned tablets were rightly criticised for being too strong, and contained hydrolyzed protein and monosodium glutamate. Tablets now have improved but I believe they are not as good as *Knorr* stockpots, now available for beef, chicken, fish or vegetable dishes. I still consider the flavours a little too strong, but they are acceptable if you only use half a stockpot.

Sauces, Mayonnaise and Vinaigrette

Many of our everyday dishes include sauces, but they are not necessarily labelled as such. Any dish using water, milk, meat juices, vegetable or fruit juices, wine, flour, salt and pepper, herbs and spices, is creating a sauce.

So, rather than go through the innumerable types of sauces here which you see in many cookbooks, I have only singled out Béchamel, Espagnole, Cheese, Tomato and Mushroom sauces, as well as Mayonnaise and Vinaigrette, which you will need to use.

Béchamel Sauce

Béchamel is a basic white sauce, to which you can add mushrooms, cheese, tomato or onion. Traditionally it is made with equal quantities of butter and flour, called a roux, with milk, herbs and spices added. The problem is that a roux takes about fifteen minutes of gentle cooking to take out the flour taste, so I mainly use cornflour, which is thinner but equally effective in thickening the sauce, and goes well if mixed with a glass of white wine, without necessarily needing milk as an ingredient.

So, to simplify the sauce, just use one teaspoon of cornflour, with one glass (4 fl oz) of dry white wine. Stir it in to whatever dish you are making, and simmer for two or three minutes until the sauce thickens. If you want a thinner sauce, just add a little more dry white wine.

Espagnole Sauce

This does use a roux (flour and butter), but the flour is allowed to brown, before adding any liquid. This tends to be used for chicken and some meat dishes, which require longer cooking times. A true Espagnole sauce (not used in these recipes) could also include carrots, mushrooms, tomatoes and even chopped bacon.

Cheese Sauce

My own recipe for cheese sauce is as follows:

1/2 oz butter
4 oz grated mature cheddar cheese
3-4 fl oz milk
Salt and milled pepper
1 tsp cornflour
2 or 3 drops of Tabasco

Mix and heat the ingredients for 3-4 minutes until the sauce is smooth and has thickened.

You can vary the thickness of the sauce by altering the kind of milk used. Blue top milk is creamier, green top a little thinner, red top a little too thin. Either add more cheese, or more milk to suit your taste. If you want the sauce richer, add a knob of blue cheese.

Tomato Sauce

1/2 oz butter
6 oz skinned tomatoes, quartered
1 level tbsp tomato purée
1 clove garlic, finely chopped
1/2 tsp basil
1/2 tsp thyme
Salt and milled pepper

1 tsp cornflour
4 tbsp dry white wine
1 tbsp cream

Soak the tomatoes in hot water and peel them.

Put tomatoes, butter, garlic and seasoning into a small pan. Bring to simmer for about 5 minutes, mash and stir. Add cornflour, wine and stir again. When sauce has thickened, add cream.

Mushroom Sauce

1/2 oz butter
6 oz mushrooms, halved and thinly sliced
Salt and milled pepper
1 tsp cornflour
2 fl oz (4 tbsp) milk
2 fl oz (4 tbsp) dry white wine

Cook mushrooms in a small pan in butter for about 3-4 minutes, until they start browning. Add seasoning, milk, cornflour and wine. Stir until sauce thickens and simmer for another minute.

Sauce Vinaigrette

Purists argue over the ratio of olive oil to vinegar - some say 6:1 some 2:1 - but they all agree on using the best olive oil. Also, it depends which vinegar you use. If you use white wine vinegar, I suggest the following:

4 tbsp olive oil
1 tbsp white wine vinegar
1 clove garlic, finely chopped
1/2 tsp Dijon mustard
1/2 tsp sugar
3 or 4 drops of Tabasco
Salt and milled pepper

Whisk all ingredients vigorously with a fork before using.

If you use Balsamic vinegar, use more than 2 tbsp of oil to 1 of vinegar, as it has a dominant taste.

Mayonnaise

They say the best mayonnaise is the one you make yourself, but you need to be patient as it takes a little time, care and effort. First of all, the ingredients need to be at room temperature, and you need a good solid mixing bowl, a whisk, or an electric blender on slow. If you use a blender, it is easier with larger quantities. My recipe is as follows:

1 egg yolk
1 clove garlic, finely chopped
1/4 tsp Dijon mustard
2-3 tsp lemon juice
4 tbsp olive oil
Salt and milled pepper

Whisk the egg yolk, garlic and mustard in a solid bowl, then add olive oil from a jug - one drop at a time - whisking vigorously for a minute or two (using a jug of oil with a fine lip). The mix should gradually thicken and go creamy.

You can then drip in a little lemon juice as you carry on mixing.

Once the process has started satisfactorily, you can increase the rate of adding olive oil to a thin stream, but be patient as it will still take several minutes.

Finally, taste the mayonnaise and add the rest of the lemon juice, whisking all the time.

Add seasoning to taste.

Wine

A lot of recipes call for one glass of dry white wine. The measure should be about four fluid ounces, so please find a suitable glass and use that, without having to measure it out each time you use these recipes. If the recipe says six ounces, use a glass and a half.

More often than not, the wine is used with cornflour as a thickening agent. If the sauce is a little too thick for you, add a little more wine.

WEIGHTS AND MEASURES CONVERSION TABLES

Weight - grams to ounces

28 g	= 1 oz
56 g	= 2 ozs
112 g	= 4 ozs
225 g	= 8 ozs
450 g	= 1 lb

Liquids - litres & millilitres to fluid ounces to spoonfuls/pints

3.5 ml	= 1/8 fl oz = 1 tsp
7 ml	= 1/4 fl oz = 1 dstsp
14 ml	= 1/2 fl oz = 1 tbsp
100 ml	= 3 1/2 fl oz
140 ml	= 5 fl oz = 1/4 pint
560 ml	= 20 fl oz = 1 pint
750 ml	= 26 fl oz = 1 bottle
1 l	= 35 fl oz

Printed in Great Britain
by Amazon.co.uk, Ltd.,
Marston Gate.